SURVIVING YOUR SATURN RETURN

A GUIDED JOURNAL TO HELP YOU THRIVE IN YOUR COSMIC COMING-OF-AGE

◆ ◆ ◆

PHOEBE FENRIR

ILLUSTRATED BY JIANAN LIU

RP STUDIO

PHILADELPHIA

RP Studio™
Hachette Book Group
1290 Avenue of the Americas, New York, NY 10104
www.runningpress.com
@Running_Press

Printed in Singapore

First Edition: February 2023

Published by RP Studio, an imprint of Perseus Books, LLC, a subsidiary of Hachette Book Group, Inc. The RP Studio name and logo are trademarks of the Hachette Book Group.

The publisher is not responsible for websites (or their content) that are not owned by the publisher.

Design by Jenna McBride

ISBN: 978-0-7624-8173-6

COS

10 9 8 7 6 5 4 3 2 1

CONTENTS

✦ ✦ ✦

✦ ✦ ✦

WHAT
AND
WHEN
IS YOUR
SATURN
RETURN?

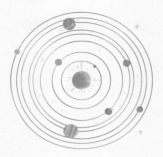

If you're reading this journal, there's a high chance that you've heard of what is commonly known as the Saturn Return. But what is this astrological event, exactly? What do people mean when they say their Saturn Return has just begun, or that they're in the middle of it?

The Saturn Return is a phenomenon that occurs when the planet has returned to the same place it was in the universe at the time of your birth. Earth takes one calendar year to make its way around the Sun, about 92 million miles away from us. Saturn is much farther from the Sun, about 794 million miles farther, and so takes a whopping *twenty-nine and a half* Earth years to orbit the Sun.

Each Saturn Return starts approximately every twenty-seven years, depending on your birth chart. Your peak Saturn Return is the period of a few months when Saturn finally comes home to the same degree in the zodiac it held when you were born. But the whole duration of your Saturn Return lasts two and a half years, when the planet is back in your natal Saturn sign. You'll deeply feel the effects of Saturn throughout this entire period.

As you navigate your Saturn Return, remember that, just as every planet proceeds through the universe in its own way and time, so do we.

Your Saturn Return is an opportunity to reflect on where you are in your life and where you're headed, a wake-up call to finally make tough decisions or changes you've been avoiding, and a chance to finally arrive at and settle into the life you've been building for yourself all along.

You may notice things coming to a head during this period. You may be in the middle of a career change, or certain relationships that you thought were solid are seeming to fall apart or fade away. Maybe you've experienced a major loss that you are struggling to recover from. Saturn Return has a reputation for being a turbulent, even punishing, time, when it can seem that everything is going wrong. But as long as you trust and use the wisdom you have gained in your life so far, you will not only survive, but thrive, until the next time Saturn visits.

This journal will help you to make the most of this time. As you work through it, you can proceed page by page, or you can jump around, sometimes moving retrograde! You can aim to complete two to three prompts each week or move at whatever pace feels most natural to you.

If you're a math person, you might be thinking that the years do not add up. If Saturn is nine and a half times farther from the Sun than we are (and its orbital path is approximately nine and a half times longer), then why does it take Saturn twenty-nine and a half, instead of nine and a half, years to orbit the Sun and return to where it was at the exact time when you were born? The answer lies in Saturn orbiting at a much slower speed. The Sun exerts less gravitational pull on Saturn, being that the planet is so far away.

Sitting down with this journal can be a powerful ritual of self-care and self-exploration. To get in the right mind-set, you might try lighting a candle, making yourself a cup of tea, or putting on relaxing or energizing music to go along with your journaling. You might also try working through this journal at the same time each  morning or evening. Or just turn to this journal whenever you have a few minutes for a reset in the middle of your day. The process of working through each prompt should feel rewarding, but if you also want to celebrate yourself with some kind of treat after you finish a prompt or section, go for it!

You enter your first Saturn Return when you're between 27 and 30 years old. Your second Saturn Return is from the ages of 56 to 59 years old. And your third Saturn Return will be when you're between 86 and 89. To calculate the exact dates of your Saturn Return, you can consult with an astrologer or use an online calculator. List the approximate dates of your Saturn Returns below.

✦ ✦

FIRST SATURN RETURN:

SECOND SATURN RETURN:

THIRD SATURN RETURN:

✦ ✦

One of the reasons that your Saturn Return lasts for so long is that Saturn (like Mercury) doesn't always seem to orbit with linear forward motion, but can sometimes appear to move retrograde. Saturn and Mercury don't *actually* move retrograde, however. They only look that way because of the way our planet Earth moves in relation to them. This fooled early astronomers, who thought Saturn and Mercury were moving backward when they weren't! During your Saturn Return, don't beat yourself up for parts of your life that might have felt like retrograde motion or stasis. Like Saturn, you *were* progressing, if elliptically.

SURVIVING

AND

THRIVING

BY

SIGN

ARIES

✦ ✦ ✦

If you're an Aries, you may have, ramlike, thrown yourself into things—lovers, projects, friendships—without always pausing to consider the best option or to seek out guidance from others. As the first sign in the zodiac, your instinct isn't always to look to others or even to your own experience for support. Consider your Saturn Return your chance to finally slow down and assess what you've learned (or failed to learn) over the past years.

TAURUS

✦ ✦ ✦

As a Taurus, you can probably think of at least one job, relationship, or living situation you've stayed in for too long. Maybe it's the one you're in right now. Or maybe you simply struggle to get out of your cozy bed in the morning or step away from whatever television show you're binging at night. While there's nothing wrong with luxuriating from time to time, you'll want to be careful about not becoming complacent. Your Saturn Return is an opportunity to evaluate whether you're moving toward your desired destination, or if you've simply let yourself become comfortable in a situation that is no longer serving you.

GEMINI

◆ ◆ ◆

If you're a Gemini, you often take on too much in your career, relationships, and community. Taking care of yourself has probably taken a backseat once or twice in the past years. Use your Saturn Return to take stock of all that you're doing. Consider what relationships, practices, and uses of your time are most nourishing to you and those you love. Winnowing down can be painful, but remember that anything you cut back on will gift you time and energy that you can use elsewhere, for yourself or your community.

CANCER

✦ ✦ ✦

As a Cancer looking back on the years leading up to your Saturn Return, you likely have at least a few grudges you haven't forgotten. Now is the time to face those grudges head on, whether that means working through them in this journal or finally talking through a conflict with a friend or family member. Your tendency is to put up walls when you feel vulnerable, but this is an opportunity to let yourself be tender, to admit your hurt, even if it's just to yourself, so that you might finally let it go.

LEO

◆ ◆ ◆

Leos like to be the life of the party. If you're a Leo who prioritizes your social life above all else—think about what being in communion with others means to you. Are other people there to satiate your ego, or because you feel truly fulfilled in their presence? There's nothing wrong with devoting much of your time to relationships, as long as they sustain instead of drain you, and as long as you give your friends and partners as much as they give you.

VIRGO

◆ ◆ ◆

As a Virgo, you may sometimes find that you focus on your friends and family to the detriment of caring for yourself. Think of your Saturn Return as an opportunity to rest, so that when you are with the people you love, you can give them your full self. A related common challenge for Virgos is wanting to fix everything that's broken within their friends' lives or greater community. During this Saturn Return, accept that while you can't immediately solve *all* the problems in your world (or in your own life!), there are small, meaningful steps you can take to heal yourself and your community. Those steps are more than enough. You are more than enough.

LIBRA

✦ ✦ ✦

Libras aspire to maintain balance in all areas of their life. You might be so devoted to pursuing balance that you don't let yourself dive completely into any one activity, role, or relationship. You might carefully consider every decision, to the point that you're paralyzed by the fear of imperfection or making the "wrong" choice. This Saturn return, trust your instincts. And once you make a decision, allow yourself to stick to it, to wholly focus your energy on where you are now.

SCORPIO

◆ ◆ ◆

If you're a Scorpio, you're known to always be plotting. You might struggle to fully experience the current moment. At work, you might constantly think about what your *next* job will be. All day, you might be distracted by thoughts of dinner. And when you're with a friend, you might get caught up in planning trips for the future, instead of enjoying your time together. Now is the time to allow yourself to become more present. Think about your Saturn Return not as a stepping-stone toward what's next, but as an opportunity to appreciate where you already are and all that you already have.

SAGITTARIUS

✦ ✦ ✦

As a Sagittarius, you're willing to make big changes and adapt to whatever upheavals come your way. While these qualities make you resilient and someone who's already experienced a ton, they might also result in a life that is not quite settled. It's time for you to evaluate where your adventures have taken you, and to ask if there are things that you've avoided dealing with by being constantly on the move. This Saturn Return, give yourself permission to feel comfortable with yourself and your life, even if you're not moving cities or making another drastic change every six months.

CAPRICORN

✦ ✦ ✦

Capricorns are ruled by Saturn, so this is an especially significant time for you, and the perfect opportunity to finally tackle or complete that one project that's been weighing on you. Serious Capricorns are known to become more playful as they get older. So, along with rolling up your sleeves as you get to work (or keep working), redefine what "play" means to you as an adult. You have time for work *and* play, and you might find great reward in letting your "work" become more playful too.

AQUARIUS

◆ ◆ ◆

As an Aquarius, you are committed to helping better your world. And while the pursuit of justice and change is necessary, you may have sometimes neglected your immediate community at the expense of a larger cause. This Saturn Return, apply the good work that you do to the people closest to you. Or, if you're feeling guilt because you haven't been an activist or advocate just yet, think about how you can finally use that Aquarius spirit to make change for yourself and the world.

PISCES

✦ ✦ ✦

For romantic and idealistic Pisces, the adjustment to adulthood (or late adulthood if this is your second or third Saturn Return) can be particularly challenging. While your passionate, youthful energy is often one of your strengths, it may sometimes prevent you from taking on responsibility or creating boundaries within your work and personal life. During your Saturn Return, focus on becoming and staying grounded.

Does your sign's advice for your Saturn Return ring true? If not, that's okay! One of the reasons that a Saturn Return is so powerful is that by the time it comes around, we're starting to know who we are and become our own best teachers. So, try writing out what you think *you* most need to hear coming into this period of growth, change, and self-reflection.

MISSION TO SATURN: PREPARING FOR LIFTOFF

Look back on all the years that led you and Saturn to this moment. What are you most grateful for?

What are you most hoping to learn about yourself during your Saturn Return?

What are you most hoping to experience or manifest during your Saturn Return?

What about this moment in your life is creating the most anxiety or stress for you?

What do you fear when you think about the years ahead?

Was there a time in the past years when you felt you were moving retrograde?

_____

_____

_____

_____

_____

_____

_____

_____

_____

_____

_____

_____

_____

_____

_____

_____

_____

_____

Consider how that "retrograde" time may have actually been healing or instructive for you. How did that experience challenge you or make you who you are today? What can you learn from that "retrograde" time now that it's in your rearview?

What changes would you like to experience during this Saturn Return?

What would you like to let go of?

What would you like to gain during your Saturn Return? This can be a practical pursuit, such as learning a new skill or something tied to your emotional life.

The Saturn Return is ultimately rewarding but not always easy. Make a list of all the people who love you and who you love. Revisit this list whenever you're feeling low and in need of support.

_____

_____

_____

_____

_____

_____

_____

_____

_____

_____

_____

_____

_____

_____

_____

_____

_____

_____

_____

Are there any memories from the past that are weighing on you? How do you plan to confront these experiences?

PURSUITS

AND

PASTIMES

Here's an exercise you may have done before. Where do you want to be in your career in five years? Define "career" in your own terms.

_____

_____

_____

_____

_____

_____

_____

_____

_____

_____

_____

_____

_____

_____

_____

_____

_____

_____

_____

In ten years?

In twenty-seven years, or by the time of your next Saturn Return?

_____

_____

_____

_____

_____

_____

_____

_____

_____

_____

_____

_____

_____

_____

_____

_____

_____

_____

Now, instead of thinking about *how* you can achieve those career goals, think about *why* you want to achieve them in the first place. How do you hope these hypothetical benchmarks will satisfy, challenge, or reward you?

_____

_____

_____

_____

_____

_____

_____

_____

_____

_____

_____

_____

_____

_____

_____

_____

_____

_____

Think about how you might achieve the most enticing parts of those career goals *now*, during *this* Saturn Return, instead of in five, ten, or twenty-seven years. You probably won't wake up tomorrow with a massive raise, or corner office, or all the creative freedom you want and deserve, but what changes in mindset or daily routine can you make now to help you get there?

Instead of trying to find all of your satisfaction within your work, where else can you find creative fulfillment in your life?

Design your ideal daily schedule, from the moment you wake up to the time you go to bed.

5 a.m.	3 p.m.
6 a.m.	4 p.m.
7 a.m.	5 p.m.
8 a.m.	6 p.m.
9 a.m.	7 p.m.
10 a.m.	8 p.m.
11 a.m.	9 p.m.
12 p.m.	10 p.m.
1 p.m.	11 p.m.
2 p.m.	12 a.m.

In the schedule you designed, did you give yourself time to relax or recharge? Did you give yourself time to transition between tasks? Did you allot time for those tasks that aren't always fun or fulfilling but do need to be completed each day (doing dishes, tidying up, answering emails, etc.)? Try another more realistic or forgiving version of your daily schedule.

5 a.m.	3 p.m.
6 a.m.	4 p.m.
7 a.m.	5 p.m.
8 a.m.	6 p.m.
9 a.m.	7 p.m.
10 a.m.	8 p.m.
11 a.m.	9 p.m.
12 p.m.	10 p.m.
1 p.m.	11 p.m.
2 p.m.	12 a.m.

What do you think the major differences are between your "ideal" schedule and how your days tend to usually go? Which differences are within your control and which are not? How can you be kind to yourself when things don't go as planned?

_____

_____

_____

_____

_____

_____

_____

_____

_____

_____

_____

_____

_____

_____

_____

_____

_____

_____

For the next week, without judgment, keep track of how you spend your time when you're not working. While you don't have to count up every single minute you spend on your phone, try to be as honest as possible. At the end of the week, reflect on how you might be more intentional with your time.

What does your dream office, workspace, or desk look like? Note: While this could be a workspace for your actual job, it could also be a workspace for what you love to do outside of work (like journaling!). Draw this dream workspace below!

What small changes can you make to your workspace today to make it more like your dream?

Is there a space in your home that feels like it's yours? If you feel like you share every space in your home with your job, family, or roommates, think about what little corner you can make yours. This space can be as small as your bed or a wall. How can you make this space feel more like a refuge or sanctuary? What little touches can you add to your current living space so that it feels more like home?

Where do you already exert creative freedom and decision-making within your current job or role? Don't undervalue the work you do every single day! How does your "personal" life nurture your career, and vice versa?

If you feel that your career is seeping into all aspects of your life in an unhealthy way, how can you create firmer boundaries and spaces that have nothing to do with work?

Make a list of hobbies or activities you've always wanted to try but have never found the time for. Also include hobbies you only partake in sporadically. How can you set aside more time for these pursuits? What about these activities brings you excitement or joy?

For the next week, try not bringing your phone or computer into your bedroom at night or checking them first thing in the morning. Also try moving a task or habit that you normally do online to good old-fashioned pen and paper. For example, you might brainstorm or make a to-do list in a notebook instead of in your notes app. Or when cooking from a recipe off the internet, try printing it out instead of referencing your phone.

Did shifting your phone or computer use this week change your perspective or ability to focus? At the end of this week, you can absolutely return to looking at your phone first thing in the morning, but do so with intention. Be mindful of how your relationship with your devices is or isn't serving you.

When did you last find the time to do absolutely nothing? Scrolling through your phone or binging your favorite show doesn't count. "Doing nothing" means letting your mind wander. And while this practice has immense benefits for your well-being, part of its power comes from stepping off the productivity treadmill. In other words, try doing nothing for nothing's sake. Even if the dishes aren't done. Even if you want to jump to the next page of this journal. Even if you want to check your phone. Go sit on the couch, on the floor, or outside and let your mind be.

Did your mind go anywhere surprising while you were doing nothing? Did you feel frustrated or anxious? Reflect on where you wandered.

_____

_____

_____

_____

_____

_____

_____

If you can, try to commit to doing nothing a few times a day or week. You can start small. Five or ten minutes here and there. As part of a regular practice, doing nothing can help you become more creative, more in touch with your emotions, and more purposeful about how you live your life and engage with others.

How does your work ("work" can mean your job or something you devote time to outside of your career) contribute to the well-being of your community or your world?

HEALTH
IS
WEALTH

What does "health" mean to you?

What kind of "health" do you aspire to that will sustain you until your next Saturn Return?

Oftentimes, we are hard on our bodies. We call ourselves "weak," and sometimes we do feel justifiably weak or tired. Life is exhausting! But one of the profound lessons of a Saturn Return is that we've survived long enough for Saturn to arc its way across our entire solar system. No matter the injuries it has endured, your body has kept on, just as Saturn has kept on orbiting.

While Saturn was traveling, where was your body taking you? List some of the places your body moved you, near and far.

Focus on one of the destinations from on the previous page. Close your eyes and try to mentally return to that place. Draw a picture of it below.

What did this place smell like? Can you describe the light?

How did your body feel in that place? What sensations did you experience? What textures? Are you cold or warm? What emotions does this place conjure?

Thank your body for taking you to that place and helping you relive it just now!

Now, keep your eyes open and focus on the moment. How does this moment, in this particular place, feel in your body? Pay enough attention that you will be able to relive this moment again during your next Saturn Return.

_____

_____

_____

_____

_____

_____

_____

_____

_____

_____

_____

_____

_____

_____

_____

_____

_____

_____

_____

_____

Try something new with your body (or something that feels new because it's been so long since you last tried it). This could be a dance move, a yoga pose, a sport, anything. Just try it once. It's okay if you fall on your face.

Reflect on how that experience of moving your body in a new way felt. Were you frustrated, nervous, or exhilarated?

_____

_____

_____

_____

_____

_____

_____

_____

_____

_____

_____

_____

_____

_____

_____

_____

Over the course of the next week (without judgment!) keep track of what time you go to sleep and what time you wake up each morning.

Monday

Rising time:

Bedtime:

Tuesday

Rising time:

Bedtime:

Wednesday

Rising time:

Bedtime:

Thursday

Rising time:

Bedtime:

Friday

Rising time:

Bedtime:

Saturday

Rising time:

Bedtime:

Sunday

Rising time:

Bedtime:

By this point in your life, you should have a decent sense of how much sleep you need each night to feel your best. Most adults need at least seven hours of sleep a night to feel and remain healthy. Many need eight or nine hours. If you've been getting by on less sleep because of a punishing schedule, can you prioritize and invest in your well-being by committing to sleeping more? How?

One powerful, simple sleep practice is to go to bed at around the same time every night and wake up around the same time every morning. Unpredictable work or family schedules can make this challenging, but if you can, try to stick to a consistent sleep schedule. If anxiety disturbs your sleep, try journaling before bed. What are some worries that keep you up at night?

Go for a thirty-minute walk around your neighborhood. As you walk, note the sensations in your body. When you return, record your observations. They can be observations of your body or of the world around you, or both!

If you were Saturn, what might have you have observed on your "walk" through the universe?

_____

_____

_____

_____

_____

_____

_____

_____

_____

_____

_____

_____

_____

_____

_____

_____

_____

_____

_____

_____

What are some of your most memorable meals from the past years? What about those meals did you enjoy? How did they nourish you physically and spiritually? What do you love to cook for yourself or your loved ones? Or if you don't cook, what's a restaurant where you would want to take your friends?

List some meals you'd like to cook or try during this Saturn Return. When you do eat those meals, savor them.

The Saturn Return is a reminder to check in with our body and our mind. It might be time to get that checkup you've been putting off. Maybe you need to go to the dentist (or finally start flossing). Whatever it is you've been avoiding, list it below. Then, make an appointment!

How do you care for your mental health?

What resources are available to you that you haven't taken advantage of yet? How can you prioritize your mental health more?

_____

_____

_____

_____

_____

_____

_____

_____

_____

_____

_____

_____

_____

_____

_____

_____

_____

_____

_____

Has your definition of "health" changed as you've worked through these pages? How?

Can you try to be "healthy" without judging yourself for how you exist in the world? Can you accept and appreciate your body and mind? List some times in your life when you felt strong. Look back on these moments when you're feeling tired or weak.

RELATIONSHIPS

What are the key relationships in your life? Describe why these loved ones are so important to you. Include favorite shared memories, qualities you appreciate, or what you love to do together.

Now, write out everyone's sign next to their name. Do you see any fun or surprising patterns about what signs you're drawn to and what signs are drawn to you?

It's time to practice gratitude for those who have helped you make it to this Saturn Return. Reflect on who you're grateful for and why. You can include the people from the previous pages. You might also add those to whom you haven't spoken in years, such as old teachers, old friends, or even strangers who were kind to you.

Take some time to let your loved ones know how much you appreciate what they've done for you. Go ahead and send some thank-you texts, emails, or handwritten letters. Draft your message below. Or pick up the phone to call your ride-or-dies and tell them how much they mean to you. This might feel awkward at first, but remember that absolutely no one will be bummed to receive a call out of the blue that says they're loved and appreciated.

Who do you most admire? This list might overlap with some of the people you've already been thinking about. Include artists, activists, or other visionaries who you don't know personally, but respect.

Choose one person from your admiration list who you know personally. Ask them how they navigated a difficult transition in their life (bonus points if this transition was their Saturn Return). What can you learn from them?

Now, choose a person you don't know from your list and research their biography.
Where were they at each of their Saturn Returns? What can you learn from them?

Find someone in your life who is also going through their Saturn Return and do a check-in with them. How can you help each other through this time and hold each other accountable as you evaluate your lives?

The work you're doing on your own journey means you're well equipped to help friends through their challenges.

Are any of the relationships in your life bringing you anxiety? How can you make those relationships more fruitful for you and the other person?

Are there any relationships in your life that you feel you've outgrown? Can those relationships shift to accommodate who you are now? Or is it time to pull away from those relationships?

_____

_____

_____

_____

_____

_____

_____

_____

_____

_____

_____

_____

_____

_____

_____

_____

_____

_____

_____

_____

Are there any old grudges that you're still holding? If so, now is the perfect time to finally work through them. Remember that Saturn Return isn't just about moving on. It's also about change. Who are you without your grudges? Who do you want to be? How can you go about becoming that person?

Is there any past behavior or conflict that *you* need to apologize for? If so, make a plan to apologize. What can you say to undo the hurt you've caused, or to make sure you won't do it again?

How can you become a more generous friend, partner, or family member?

_____
_____
_____
_____
_____
_____
_____
_____
_____
_____
_____
_____
_____
_____
_____
_____
_____
_____
_____
_____

What haven't you forgiven yourself for? Can you forgive yourself now? Be as generous and accepting of yourself as you are of your friends.

While so much of Saturn Return is about the challenging work of taking stock, it's also the perfect time for fresh experiences and growth. Making new friends in adulthood can be hard, but this month try to meet someone new.

_____

_____

_____

_____

_____

_____

_____

_____

_____

_____

_____

_____

_____

_____

_____

_____

Casual friendships can be fulfilling and joyful. Instead of setting out to find a new best friend, try simply waving or saying hello to a neighbor you've never spoken to before. Sometimes even the smallest interactions do eventually lead to new best friends.

Make a list of new activities to try with a friend, romantic partner, or family member. Keep track of those experiences here.

WEALTH
IS
HEALTH

What does "wealth" mean to you? What kind of "wealth" do you aspire to? Think beyond the numbers in your bank account. Wealth can mean having money, but it can also mean enjoying relationships, physical health, or knowledge.

In what aspect of your life do you most want to build wealth as you've defined it? In other words, what part of your life is currently feeling fallow and in need of attention?

Think about *why* you want this form of wealth. Is there something in particular you wish you could afford? Or are you longing for an increased sense of security?

What is your relationship with money? How would you like your spending habits to change as you settle into this next phase of your life? What does money give you?

_____

_____

_____

_____

_____

_____

_____

_____

_____

_____

_____

_____

_____

_____

_____

_____

_____

_____

_____

_____

_____

If you had a million dollars, how would you spend it?

Which of these things do you want versus need? Which of these things do you already have?

How can you strike a balance between appreciating what you have and aspiring to have more in the future?

What kind of generational wealth would you like to create for your children, your potential future children, or the members of your community who will follow you?

_____

_____

_____

_____

_____

_____

_____

_____

_____

_____

_____

_____

_____

_____

_____

_____

_____

_____

_____

_____

We've all been jealous of what friends, colleagues, or celebrities have that we don't. Sometimes we lose sight of what we have. What about your life might others envy?

_____

_____

_____

_____

_____

_____

_____

_____

_____

_____

_____

_____

_____

_____

_____

Now is a great time to cleanse your social media feeds. Try spending less time on apps that make you sad (or leave you wanting to spend money). You can also mute or unfollow people or accounts that make you particularly envious.

When was the last time you were jealous of someone? Try imagining what their social media feed doesn't show. What about their life might be challenging?

What kinds of communal wealth can you pool with the people around you? Ideas: Trade old clothes or items, participate in a skill share, go in with friends for a vacation or a night out.

_____

_____

_____

_____

_____

_____

_____

_____

_____

_____

_____

_____

_____

_____

_____

_____

_____

What systems of wealth in your community or country are unjust?

How can you advocate for change within or help correct those systems?

How are you already "wealthy"? Think about the possessions you most value and why. Also think about valuable friendships, a place you cherish, or something in your heart that makes you feel you have enough.

How can you nurture these resources until your next Saturn Return?

COMMUNITY

Saturn has a whopping *eighty-two* estimated moons that are also returning to the place in the zodiac that they held at the moment when you were born. Saturn and its many moons are orbiting our solar system amid all the other planets, along with asteroids, comets, and meteors.

Like Saturn, you move within a community, sometimes orbited by others, sometimes orbiting.

What does "community" mean to you?

_____

_____

_____

_____

_____

_____

_____

_____

_____

_____

_____

_____

_____

_____

Draw your own solar system. Who is in your galaxy, your broader universe?

List all the communities you consider yourself a part of.

What do you give to your communities? What do they give to you?

Remember a time in the past when you keenly felt a sense of community or belonging. Describe that moment. What was special about it?

Do you overly rely on your community for your sense of self? Think about who you are apart from the larger systems that you fit into. And remember, it's okay to be a lone wolf every now and then.

What can you do to make your communities more inclusive and supportive of people from all backgrounds and walks of life?

Did you list the natural world as one of your communities? You share your corner of the earth with plants, animals, and insects. You are a part of the natural world. How can you help that world thrive for the next twenty-seven years?

_____

_____

_____

_____

_____

_____

_____

_____

_____

_____

IDEAS

+ Plant a tree! If you don't have a yard, there are often programs in cities to plant trees in your closest curb strip or park. As you care for the tree, think about how big it will become by the time of your next Saturn Return.

+ Join or start a weekly or monthly trash cleanup.

+ Volunteer with a local nature conservation organization or get involved in climate change advocacy.

+ Feed your local birds.

What works of art are or were most meaningful to you?

Return to a work of art (a song, a book, a movie, etc.) that you loved when you were younger but haven't experienced in years. How does it strike you now?

Building community takes time. Sharing what we love with others is one step in that direction.

Share one of the works of art you listed previously with someone who might appreciate it. What was their reaction?

Every time you purchase anything, you have an impact on a community. What communities would you like to support? Think about them the next time you're making a purchase.

SHOP LOCAL

If you want to be more politically engaged, don't overlook local politics and elections as a way to make a difference. Set some goals for becoming a more active citizen, whether that's attending a town hall, voting in the next local election, or joining a book club to finally meet your neighbors.

How do you think community work might inform your personal growth during your Saturn Return?

_____

_____

_____

_____

_____

_____

_____

_____

_____

_____

_____

_____

_____

_____

_____

_____

_____

_____

_____

_____

_____

MISSION ACCOMPLISHED
. . . OR
ONGOING!

Return to your hopes from the beginning of this journal. How have those hopes changed or not changed? What new hopes do you have now?

What progress do you feel you've made toward those hopes, or toward different aspirations if you changed course along the way?

What hopes still feel far away? What's stopping you from reaching them? What is and isn't within your control?

What are you most proud of yourself for? Take some time to celebrate yourself.

Return to your stressors and fears from the beginning of the journal. Are those feelings still heavy for you? Or have they changed?

After you're finished reflecting, tear those pages from the beginning out. Read them one last time. Thank your fears and regrets for any action they might have spurred, anything they may have taught you about yourself. Now, crumple them up and throw them away (or recycle them). Let them go.

This week, every night before bed, track what you're most grateful for about each day.

Monday

I'm grateful for _____

_____

_____

_____

Tuesday

I'm grateful for _____

_____

_____

_____

Wednesday

I'm grateful for _____

_____

_____

_____

Thursday

I'm grateful for _____

_____

_____

_____

Friday

I'm grateful for _____

_____

_____

_____

Saturday

I'm grateful for _____

_____

_____

_____

Sunday

I'm grateful for _____

_____

_____

_____

Think of a mantra to return to throughout the rest of your Saturn Return and the years ahead, as you embark on another journey around the Sun. Write your uplifting words over and over again (in different styles, if you'd like!) until the entire spread is filled, or use one of the following quotes as your mantra.

"Luxury is to be able to take control of one's life, health, and the pursuit of happiness in a way that is joyful."

—ANDRÉ LEON TALLEY

"You are your best thing."

—TONI MORRISON

"To pay attention, this is our endless and proper work."

—MARY OLIVER

Tonight, after the sun sets, go outside and try to find Saturn in the night sky. How does it feel to connect with this planet? If you live in a city with too much light pollution for you to make out Saturn, try going to a planetarium show instead. Or simply do some research on Saturn and jot down what you learn. What do you think about this powerful being?

What are some things you loved to do as a child that you haven't done in years (e.g., catching falling leaves, watching clouds, any form of play)?

Return to at least one of these activities and write about the experience. The Saturn Return is about growth, and sometimes that means regaining parts of yourself that you've lost. You're never too old to play.

_____

_____

_____

_____

_____

_____

_____

_____

_____

_____

_____

_____

_____

_____

_____

_____

_____

_____

_____

Plan a Saturn Return party for yourself. Make it space-themed and invite friends over, or make it a private ritual. How do you want to celebrate your journey with Saturn, having traveled so far that you've cycled back to the place where your life began?

Write a letter to yourself to be read at the time of your next Saturn Return. Think about who you want to be based on what you like about yourself right now.

Thank yourself for the work you've done over the course of this journal and your Saturn Return. What have you found within yourself that will help you survive and thrive the next time you're in transition?

CERTIFICATE
OF COMPLETION

THIS CERTIFIES THAT

_____

HAS SUCCESSFULLY SURVIVED THEIR

SATURN RETURN

_____

DATE